AI Goldmine
8 Strategies to Profit from Artificial Intelligence

By

Jackson Reed

Table of Contents

Chapter 5: Creating AI-Driven Digital Products

- Types of AI-Driven Products
- Product Development and Design
- Market Research and Validation
- Launching and Marketing Your Product

Chapter 6: Monetizing AI Content Creation

- Creating and Selling AI Content
- Leveraging AI for Blogging and Social Media
- Developing AI Tools and Apps for Content Creation
- Pricing Strategies and Revenue Models

Chapter 7: Building and Selling AI Models

- Developing Custom AI Models
- Platforms for Selling AI Models
- Licensing and Intellectual Property
- Marketing and Scaling Your AI Models

Chapter 8: AI-Powered Consulting Services

- Defining Your Consulting Niche
- Developing AI Solutions for Clients
- Building a Consulting Business
- Case Studies and Success Stories

Chapter 9: Investing in AI Startups

- Identifying Promising AI Startups
- Evaluating Investment Opportunities
- Strategies for Investing in AI
- Risk Management and Portfolio Diversification

Chapter 10: AI in E-Commerce and Dropshipping

Chapter 1: Introduction to AI and Its Potential

Understanding Artificial Intelligence

Artificial Intelligence (AI) is no longer a concept confined to science fiction. It has become an integral part of our daily lives, transforming industries and reshaping how we interact with technology. But what exactly is AI? At its core, AI refers to the capability of a machine to imitate intelligent human behavior. This can range from simple tasks like recognizing speech to more complex processes like making decisions or understanding natural language.

A Brief History of AI

The idea of AI dates back to ancient myths and legends, where artificial beings were crafted to exhibit human-like qualities. However, the modern field of AI began in the 1950s with pioneers such as Alan Turing, who proposed the concept of a machine that could simulate any human intelligence. Since then, AI has evolved through various stages, from early symbolic AI to the more advanced machine learning and deep learning systems of today.

Key AI Technologies

To understand AI's potential, it's essential to grasp the core technologies driving its development:

1. **Machine Learning (ML):** This subset of AI involves training algorithms to learn from and make predictions or decisions based on data. For example,

recommendation systems on streaming platforms use ML to suggest content based on your viewing history.

2. **Natural Language Processing (NLP):** NLP enables machines to understand and interact with human language. Virtual assistants like Siri and Alexa rely on NLP to process and respond to voice commands.

3. **Computer Vision:** This technology allows machines to interpret and make sense of visual information from the world, such as identifying objects in images or videos. It's used in applications ranging from facial recognition to autonomous vehicles.

4. **Robotics:** Robotics combines AI with physical machines to perform tasks in the real world. Examples include robotic vacuum cleaners and manufacturing robots.

AI's Transformative Potential

The potential of AI is vast and multifaceted, impacting various aspects of life and business. Here's how AI is transforming different domains:

- **Healthcare:** AI is revolutionizing diagnostics, personalized medicine, and patient care. Algorithms can analyze medical images with remarkable accuracy, predict patient outcomes, and even assist in drug discovery.
- **Finance:** In finance, AI algorithms are used for fraud detection, algorithmic trading, and customer service through chatbots. AI's ability to analyze vast amounts of data helps in making informed investment decisions.
- **Retail:** AI enhances customer experiences through personalized recommendations, inventory management, and efficient supply chain logistics.

- **Education:** AI-powered tools offer personalized learning experiences, automate administrative tasks, and provide insights into student performance.

Why AI Matters for You

Understanding and leveraging AI is not just for tech enthusiasts or professionals; it has practical implications for anyone looking to improve their financial situation or career prospects. The ability to harness AI effectively can lead to significant personal and professional growth. Whether you're interested in starting a new venture, enhancing your current business, or simply exploring new opportunities, AI offers a wealth of possibilities.

Looking Ahead

As AI continues to advance, its potential will only grow. Innovations in AI are expected to drive new industries, create novel job opportunities, and solve complex problems that were once thought insurmountable. Embracing AI today positions you to be at the forefront of these changes, ready to capitalize on emerging trends and technologies.

In the following chapters, we will explore how you can leverage AI to create tangible financial opportunities and transform your life. From freelance work to entrepreneurial ventures, the possibilities are vast and exciting. So, let's dive into the world of AI and discover how it can be a game-changer for you.

Chapter 2: Understanding AI Technologies

The Foundation of AI Technologies

To harness the power of AI, it's crucial to understand the core technologies that underpin it. These technologies drive the capabilities of AI systems and enable them to perform a range of tasks from simple automation to complex decision-making. This chapter will provide a comprehensive overview of the key AI technologies: Machine Learning, Natural Language Processing, Computer Vision, and Robotics.

Machine Learning (ML)

Machine Learning is the backbone of many modern AI systems. It involves training algorithms to learn patterns and make predictions based on data. Here's a closer look:

- **Supervised Learning:** Involves training a model on a labeled dataset, where the correct answers are provided. For example, a model can learn to identify images of cats and dogs if it is trained with labeled images of each.
- **Unsupervised Learning:** Deals with unlabeled data and aims to find hidden patterns or groupings. For instance, clustering algorithms can group similar customer behaviors together without prior knowledge of categories.
- **Reinforcement Learning:** This technique involves training models through rewards and penalties. It's commonly used in robotics and game AI, where the model learns optimal actions through trial and error.

Natural Language Processing (NLP)

NLP enables machines to understand and interact with human language. It encompasses several technologies and techniques:

- **Text Analysis:** Involves extracting meaningful information from text, such as sentiment analysis or topic modeling. For example, analyzing customer reviews to gauge overall sentiment about a product.
- **Speech Recognition:** Converts spoken language into text. It's used in virtual assistants like Google Assistant and transcription services.
- **Machine Translation:** Automatically translates text from one language to another. Services like Google Translate leverage this technology to bridge language barriers.
- **Conversational AI:** Powers chatbots and virtual assistants, enabling them to engage in human-like dialogue. These systems use NLP to understand queries and generate appropriate responses.

Computer Vision

Computer Vision allows machines to interpret and understand visual information from the world. It involves:

- **Image Classification:** Identifying objects within an image and assigning labels. For example, recognizing different types of animals in photographs.
- **Object Detection:** Detecting and locating objects within an image. This is used in applications like autonomous driving, where vehicles need to identify pedestrians and other vehicles.
- **Image Segmentation:** Dividing an image into segments to analyze parts separately. This technique is

used in medical imaging to identify and analyze tumors or other anomalies.

Robotics

Robotics combines AI with physical machines to perform tasks in the real world. Key aspects include:

- **Autonomous Robots:** Machines capable of performing tasks without human intervention. Examples include drones for aerial surveys and robotic vacuum cleaners.
- **Industrial Robots:** Used in manufacturing and assembly lines to automate repetitive tasks. They enhance precision and efficiency in production processes.
- **Collaborative Robots (Cobots):** Designed to work alongside humans in a shared workspace, assisting with tasks and improving productivity.

Integrating AI Technologies

The real power of AI comes from integrating these technologies to create sophisticated systems. For example, an AI-powered self-driving car combines computer vision to detect obstacles, machine learning to make driving decisions, and NLP to understand voice commands.

Applications Across Industries

Understanding these technologies provides insight into their diverse applications:

- **Healthcare:** AI technologies are used for diagnostic imaging, predictive analytics, and personalized medicine.

- **Finance:** Applications include fraud detection, automated trading systems, and customer service chatbots.
- **Retail:** AI enhances inventory management, personalized recommendations, and customer interactions.

Looking Forward

As AI technologies continue to advance, their capabilities and applications will expand, offering new opportunities for innovation and growth. By grasping these foundational technologies, you'll be better equipped to explore how they can be leveraged for personal and professional success.

In the next chapter, we will explore how AI is integrated into everyday life and its current impact, setting the stage for understanding its potential in creating financial opportunities.

Chapter 3: AI in Everyday Life

The Ubiquity of AI

Artificial Intelligence is seamlessly woven into the fabric of our daily lives, often operating behind the scenes to enhance convenience, efficiency, and personalization. While many people may not always recognize it, AI is influencing a wide range of activities, from how we communicate to how we shop and manage our health. This chapter explores how AI has become an integral part of everyday life and examines its various applications.

AI in Communication

AI has transformed the way we communicate in several ways:

- **Smart Assistants:** Virtual assistants like Siri, Google Assistant, and Alexa are powered by AI algorithms that process natural language to provide information, set reminders, and control smart home devices. These assistants use NLP and machine learning to understand and respond to user queries in real-time.
- **Email Filtering:** AI-driven algorithms sort and prioritize emails, filtering out spam and categorizing messages based on content and user preferences. This helps streamline communication and ensure important messages are not overlooked.
- **Language Translation:** AI-powered translation services, such as Google Translate, break down language barriers by providing real-time translation of text and speech. This technology is invaluable for

travelers, business professionals, and individuals communicating across different languages.

AI in Entertainment

AI plays a significant role in shaping our entertainment experiences:

- **Content Recommendations:** Streaming platforms like Netflix and Spotify use AI to analyze viewing or listening habits and recommend personalized content. Algorithms track user behavior and preferences to suggest movies, shows, and music that align with individual tastes.
- **Gaming:** AI enhances video games by creating intelligent, adaptive opponents and dynamic game environments. It also personalizes gaming experiences based on player behavior and preferences.
- **Creative Tools:** AI tools are now being used to create art, music, and even write stories. Platforms like DALL-E and Jukedeck use AI to generate creative content, allowing users to explore new artistic possibilities.

AI in Shopping and Retail

AI has revolutionized the shopping experience both online and offline:

- **Personalized Shopping:** E-commerce sites leverage AI to offer personalized recommendations based on browsing history, purchase patterns, and demographic data. This enhances the shopping experience by highlighting products that are most relevant to individual preferences.

- **Chatbots and Customer Service:** AI-driven chatbots handle customer inquiries, provide product information, and resolve issues around the clock. These chatbots use NLP to understand and respond to customer queries, improving response times and customer satisfaction.
- **Inventory Management:** Retailers use AI to optimize inventory levels, forecast demand, and manage supply chains. AI helps predict which products will be in high demand, reducing stockouts and excess inventory.

AI in Health and Wellness

AI is making significant strides in health and wellness:

- **Health Monitoring:** Wearable devices, such as fitness trackers and smartwatches, use AI to monitor health metrics like heart rate, activity levels, and sleep patterns. These devices provide insights and recommendations to improve overall health.
- **Telemedicine:** AI-powered platforms facilitate remote consultations with healthcare professionals. They analyze patient data and provide diagnostic support, making healthcare more accessible and efficient.
- **Personalized Medicine:** AI analyzes genetic information and medical history to tailor treatment plans for individuals. This approach, known as precision medicine, aims to optimize treatment effectiveness and minimize side effects.

AI in Transportation

AI is transforming transportation with advancements that enhance safety and efficiency:

- **Navigation Systems:** AI-powered navigation apps, such as Google Maps and Waze, provide real-time traffic updates, route optimization, and estimated arrival times. These systems use AI to analyze traffic patterns and suggest the fastest routes.
- **Autonomous Vehicles:** Self-driving cars and drones rely on AI to navigate and make driving decisions. While fully autonomous vehicles are still in development, AI technology is already being used to assist drivers with features like adaptive cruise control and lane-keeping assistance.
- **Ride-Sharing Services:** AI algorithms optimize ride-sharing and taxi services by matching passengers with drivers, predicting demand, and calculating fares. This improves efficiency and convenience for both drivers and passengers.

AI in Home Automation

Home automation systems powered by AI make daily living more convenient:

- **Smart Home Devices:** AI-enabled devices like smart thermostats, lighting systems, and security cameras adjust settings based on user preferences and habits. They can be controlled remotely and learn from user behavior to enhance comfort and security.
- **Voice Control:** AI-powered voice assistants control various smart home devices, allowing users to manage their home environment with simple voice commands.

Conclusion

AI's integration into everyday life enhances convenience, personalization, and efficiency across numerous domains. From communication and entertainment to shopping and healthcare, AI technologies are making significant impacts that improve our quality of life. Understanding these applications not only demonstrates the pervasive nature of AI but also sets the stage for exploring its potential to generate financial opportunities.

In the next chapter, we will delve into how individuals can leverage AI skills for freelancing opportunities, providing actionable insights for those looking to capitalize on the growing demand for AI expertise.

Chapter 4: Freelancing with AI Skills

The Rise of AI Freelancing

As AI continues to revolutionize various industries, the demand for AI skills has surged, creating ample opportunities for freelancers. Whether you're a data scientist, a machine learning engineer, or an AI enthusiast with technical skills, freelancing in AI offers the flexibility to work on diverse projects and collaborate with clients worldwide. This chapter explores how to leverage AI skills in the freelancing world and provides practical guidance to get started.

Identifying Your AI Skills

Before diving into freelancing, it's important to assess and identify your specific AI skills. Key areas include:

- **Data Analysis:** Proficiency in analyzing and interpreting complex data sets using tools like Python, R, or SQL.
- **Machine Learning:** Knowledge of algorithms and techniques for building predictive models, including supervised and unsupervised learning.
- **Natural Language Processing (NLP):** Expertise in working with text data, including sentiment analysis, language translation, and chatbot development.
- **Computer Vision:** Skills in image processing, object detection, and image classification using libraries such as OpenCV or TensorFlow.

- **AI Development Tools:** Familiarity with AI frameworks and platforms like TensorFlow, PyTorch, Keras, and Scikit-Learn.

Finding Freelance Opportunities

Several platforms and strategies can help you find AI freelancing opportunities:

- **Freelance Marketplaces:** Websites like Upwork, Freelancer, and Toptal offer a range of AI-related projects. Create a compelling profile highlighting your skills and previous work to attract potential clients.
- **AI-Specific Platforms:** Platforms like Kaggle and DataCamp not only offer competitions and courses but also provide networking opportunities with industry professionals looking for freelance talent.
- **Networking and Referrals:** Join AI communities and forums, attend industry conferences, and engage with professionals on LinkedIn. Building a network can lead to referrals and direct job offers.
- **Job Boards:** Explore AI-focused job boards like AIJobs, AngelList, and Stack Overflow Jobs. These platforms often feature freelance and contract positions.

Crafting Your Freelance Portfolio

A strong portfolio is essential for showcasing your expertise and attracting clients. Here's how to build one:

- **Showcase Projects:** Include detailed case studies of AI projects you've worked on, highlighting the problem, solution, and impact. Provide examples of your work, such as data visualizations, models, or applications.

- **Highlight Skills:** Emphasize your technical skills, such as proficiency in programming languages, AI frameworks, and specific techniques. Include certifications or courses that validate your expertise.
- **Client Testimonials:** Gather testimonials from previous clients or colleagues to add credibility and demonstrate your ability to deliver results.

Setting Up Your Freelance Business

Establishing a successful freelance business involves more than just technical skills. Consider the following:

- **Defining Your Niche:** Focus on a specific area of AI where you excel, such as NLP or computer vision. Specializing can help you stand out in a competitive market and attract clients looking for expertise in that area.
- **Pricing Your Services:** Research industry rates for freelance AI work and set competitive prices. Consider offering different pricing models, such as hourly rates, fixed-price projects, or retainer agreements.
- **Contract and Legal Considerations:** Draft clear contracts outlining project scope, deadlines, payment terms, and intellectual property rights. Use freelance contract templates or consult a legal professional to ensure all aspects are covered.
- **Managing Projects:** Utilize project management tools like Trello or Asana to track tasks, deadlines, and communication. Keeping projects organized helps ensure timely delivery and client satisfaction.

Building Client Relationships

Developing strong client relationships is key to a successful freelancing career:

- **Effective Communication:** Maintain clear and regular communication with clients. Provide updates, ask for feedback, and address any concerns promptly.
- **Delivering Value:** Focus on delivering high-quality work that meets or exceeds client expectations. Going the extra mile can lead to repeat business and referrals.
- **Soliciting Feedback:** After project completion, request feedback from clients to improve your services and address any areas for growth.

Scaling Your Freelance Business

As you gain experience and build a reputation, consider strategies for scaling your freelancing business:

- **Expanding Services:** Offer additional services or specialize in emerging AI trends to attract a broader client base.
- **Hiring Collaborators:** As demand grows, you might consider collaborating with other freelancers or hiring additional help to manage larger projects.
- **Building a Brand:** Develop a personal brand through a professional website, blog, or social media presence to enhance your visibility and attract more clients.

Conclusion

Freelancing with AI skills presents an exciting opportunity to work on cutting-edge projects and shape the future of technology. By leveraging your expertise, building a strong portfolio, and establishing a solid business foundation, you can create a successful freelancing career in the dynamic field of AI.

In the next chapter, we will explore how to create and monetize AI-driven digital products, offering insights into turning your AI skills into innovative and profitable solutions.

Chapter 5: Creating AI-Driven Digital Products

The Rise of AI-Driven Products

AI-driven digital products are reshaping industries and creating new opportunities for innovation and profit. By integrating AI technologies into digital products, you can offer unique solutions that address specific needs and enhance user experiences. This chapter will guide you through the process of developing AI-driven digital products, from concept to commercialization.

Identifying Opportunities

The first step in creating AI-driven products is to identify opportunities where AI can add value. Consider the following areas:

- **Problem-Solving:** Look for problems or inefficiencies in existing products or services that AI could solve. For example, an AI-powered tool that automates repetitive tasks or provides advanced analytics can offer significant benefits.
- **Market Research:** Conduct market research to understand current trends, user needs, and gaps in the market. Identify areas where AI can provide a competitive advantage or create new opportunities.
- **Customer Pain Points:** Engage with potential users to understand their pain points and needs. AI products that address real challenges are more likely to succeed.

Developing Your AI Product

Once you've identified an opportunity, follow these steps to develop your AI-driven digital product:

- **Conceptualization:** Define the core functionality and features of your product. Determine how AI will be integrated and what specific technologies (e.g., machine learning, NLP, computer vision) will be used.
- **Prototyping:** Create a prototype or minimum viable product (MVP) to validate your concept. This initial version should include the essential features and demonstrate the AI capabilities of your product.
- **Data Collection and Preparation:** AI products often rely on large datasets to train models and make predictions. Collect and prepare relevant data, ensuring it is high-quality and representative of the problem you're addressing.
- **Model Development:** Develop and train AI models using appropriate frameworks and libraries. Fine-tune the models to achieve the desired performance and accuracy.
- **Integration:** Integrate the AI models into your digital product, ensuring they work seamlessly with other components and provide a smooth user experience.
- **Testing:** Rigorously test your product to identify and fix any issues. Conduct usability testing to ensure the product meets user expectations and performs well under real-world conditions.

Monetizing Your AI Product

There are various strategies to monetize your AI-driven digital product:

- **Subscription Model:** Offer your product as a subscription service, charging users a recurring fee for access. This model works well for products with ongoing value or regular updates.

- **Freemium Model:** Provide a basic version of your product for free and offer premium features or advanced capabilities as paid upgrades. This approach can attract a large user base and convert a portion of users into paying customers.
- **One-Time Purchase:** Charge a one-time fee for purchasing your product. This model is suitable for products that offer significant value upfront without requiring ongoing maintenance or updates.
- **Licensing:** License your AI technology to other companies or developers. This can generate revenue by allowing others to integrate your technology into their products.
- **Advertising:** If your product has a large user base, you can generate revenue through in-app advertising or partnerships with other businesses.

Marketing and Launching Your Product

Effective marketing and launch strategies are crucial for the success of your AI-driven product:

- **Target Audience:** Define your target audience and tailor your marketing efforts to reach them. Use channels such as social media, content marketing, and email campaigns to generate interest.
- **Product Launch:** Plan a strategic launch to build momentum and attract early adopters. Consider hosting a launch event, running promotional campaigns, or offering limited-time discounts.
- **User Feedback:** Collect and analyze user feedback to make improvements and address any issues. Engaging with users helps build trust and ensures that your product meets their needs.

Scaling and Improving Your Product

As your product gains traction, focus on scaling and continuous improvement:

- **Scaling Infrastructure:** Ensure your infrastructure can handle increased demand as your user base grows. Optimize performance and reliability to provide a consistent user experience.
- **Feature Enhancements:** Continuously enhance your product by adding new features, improving AI models, and incorporating user feedback. Regular updates keep your product competitive and relevant.
- **Expansion:** Explore opportunities to expand your product into new markets or applications. Consider partnerships or integrations with other products to reach a broader audience.

Legal and Ethical Considerations

When developing AI-driven products, consider the following legal and ethical aspects:

- **Data Privacy:** Ensure compliance with data protection regulations and safeguard user data. Implement robust security measures to protect sensitive information.
- **Ethical AI:** Address ethical considerations related to AI, such as bias and fairness. Ensure your AI models are transparent and do not perpetuate discrimination or harm.
- **Intellectual Property:** Protect your intellectual property by securing patents, trademarks, or copyrights for your product and technology.

Conclusion

Creating AI-driven digital products offers exciting opportunities for innovation and business growth. By identifying market needs, developing robust AI solutions, and implementing effective monetization strategies, you can bring impactful products to market and drive success in the dynamic world of AI.

In the next chapter, we will explore how to monetize AI content creation, providing insights into leveraging AI for generating valuable and profitable content.

Chapter 6: Monetizing AI Content Creation

The Power of AI in Content Creation

AI is transforming the content creation landscape, offering tools and technologies that streamline the production of high-quality, engaging content. From writing articles to generating multimedia, AI can enhance creativity and efficiency, enabling individuals and businesses to generate revenue through innovative content strategies. This chapter will explore various ways to monetize AI-driven content creation and leverage these technologies for financial gain.

AI-Driven Content Creation Tools

Several AI tools can assist in creating and monetizing content:

- **Text Generation:** AI-powered platforms like GPT-4 can generate articles, blog posts, and marketing copy based on specific prompts or topics. These tools can help produce high volumes of content quickly, catering to different niches and audiences.
- **Content Optimization:** Tools such as Grammarly and Hemingway use AI to improve readability, grammar, and SEO of written content. They can help ensure that content meets high-quality standards and ranks well in search engines.
- **Image and Video Generation:** AI tools like DALL-E and Runway can create and edit images and videos. These tools enable users to produce unique visual content for social media, advertising, and websites.

- **Voice Synthesis:** AI-driven voice generation platforms like Descript and Synthesia can create realistic voiceovers for videos, podcasts, and audiobooks, reducing the need for traditional recording methods.

Monetization Strategies for AI Content

Here are various strategies to monetize content created with AI tools:

1. **Freelance Content Creation:**
   - **Client Projects:** Offer your AI-generated content services to clients in need of articles, blog posts, social media updates, or marketing materials. Platforms like Upwork and Fiverr are ideal for finding freelance opportunities.
   - **Content Agencies:** Partner with content agencies that require large volumes of content. Your AI tools can help meet tight deadlines and high production demands.
2. **Content Subscription Services:**
   - **Premium Blogs or Newsletters:** Create a subscription-based blog or newsletter that delivers AI-generated content on specific topics. Charge users a recurring fee for access to exclusive insights and updates.
   - **Membership Sites:** Build a membership site offering premium AI-generated content, such as industry reports, research papers, or educational materials.
3. **Affiliate Marketing:**
   - **Content Integration:** Incorporate affiliate links into your AI-generated content. Promote products or services relevant to your audience and earn commissions on sales generated through your links.

- Review Sites: Develop AI-driven review sites or comparison platforms that guide users to purchase decisions. Use affiliate marketing to monetize your recommendations.

4. **Ad Revenue and Sponsorships:**
   - **Monetized Blogs and YouTube Channels:** Create AI-driven blogs or YouTube channels and monetize them through ad revenue and sponsorships. AI tools can help produce engaging content that attracts a large audience.
   - **Sponsored Content:** Collaborate with brands to create sponsored content using AI-generated materials. Charge fees for featuring their products or services in your content.

5. **E-books and Digital Products:**
   - **AI-Generated E-books:** Use AI tools to write and publish e-books on topics of interest. Sell these e-books through platforms like Amazon Kindle Direct Publishing or your own website.
   - **Online Courses and Tutorials:** Develop AI-generated online courses or tutorials and sell them on platforms like Udemy or Teachable. Use AI to create course content, including written materials and multimedia elements.

6. **Content Licensing:**
   - **Stock Content:** Create and license AI-generated stock images, videos, or audio clips through stock content platforms like Shutterstock or Adobe Stock. Earn royalties whenever your content is purchased or used.
   - **White-Label Solutions:** Offer AI-generated content solutions to other businesses as white-label products. Allow them to rebrand and sell your content as their own.

Scaling AI Content Creation

To maximize your revenue potential, consider these strategies for scaling your AI content creation efforts:

- **Automated Workflows:** Implement automated content generation workflows to produce large volumes of content efficiently. Use scheduling tools to manage and publish content consistently.
- **Diversification:** Explore various content formats and platforms to reach different audiences. Combine written content with video, audio, and interactive elements to enhance engagement.
- **Team Expansion:** As demand grows, consider expanding your team with additional freelance writers, designers, or marketers. Collaborate with other experts to scale content production and diversify offerings.
- **Data-Driven Insights:** Use analytics tools to track content performance and audience engagement. Analyze data to refine your content strategy and optimize monetization efforts.

Ethical Considerations

While leveraging AI for content creation offers numerous opportunities, it's essential to address ethical considerations:

- **Content Authenticity:** Ensure transparency about AI-generated content to maintain trust with your audience. Clearly disclose when content is produced by AI, especially in sensitive or factual contexts.
- **Quality Control:** Implement quality control measures to ensure that AI-generated content meets high standards and is free from errors or biases. Regularly review and edit content as needed.

Conclusion

Monetizing AI-driven content creation opens up exciting opportunities for generating income through innovative and scalable solutions. By leveraging AI tools and implementing effective monetization strategies, you can create valuable content, attract audiences, and build a profitable content-based business.

In the next chapter, we will explore the creation and marketing of AI-powered digital products, providing insights into turning your AI skills into successful entrepreneurial ventures.

Chapter 7: Building and Selling AI Models

The Growing Market for AI Models

As AI technology advances, there is an increasing demand for specialized AI models that solve specific problems or enhance existing systems. Building and selling AI models can be a lucrative venture, offering opportunities to monetize your expertise and contribute valuable solutions to various industries. This chapter will guide you through the process of creating, refining, and commercializing AI models.

Understanding the AI Model Development Process

Before diving into the commercialization aspects, it's important to understand the fundamental steps involved in building AI models:

1. **Problem Definition:**
    - **Identify the Problem:** Determine the specific problem or need your AI model will address. This could range from image recognition to predictive analytics or natural language processing.
    - **Define Objectives:** Clearly define the objectives and success criteria for your model. Establish what performance metrics will indicate success.
2. **Data Collection and Preparation:**
    - **Gather Data:** Collect relevant and high-quality data needed to train your model. This could

involve scraping data, using public datasets, or acquiring proprietary data.

- o **Data Cleaning:** Clean and preprocess the data to remove inconsistencies, handle missing values, and normalize data formats. High-quality data is crucial for building effective models.

3. **Model Development:**
   - o **Select Algorithms:** Choose appropriate algorithms and techniques based on your problem. This might involve machine learning algorithms, neural networks, or other AI methodologies.
   - o **Training and Tuning:** Train your model using the prepared data and tune hyperparameters to optimize performance. Use techniques like cross-validation to ensure robustness.

4. **Evaluation and Testing:**
   - o **Assess Performance:** Evaluate your model using relevant metrics (e.g., accuracy, precision, recall) to ensure it meets the defined objectives.
   - o **Iterate and Improve:** Continuously refine your model based on evaluation results. Iterate through the development cycle to enhance performance and address any issues.

5. **Deployment:**
   - o **Integration:** Integrate the model into a deployment environment where it can be used by end-users or other systems. Ensure it operates efficiently and scales as needed.
   - o **Monitoring:** Implement monitoring tools to track the model's performance in real-world conditions and address any issues that arise.

Monetizing AI Models

There are several ways to monetize AI models, depending on your target market and business model:

1. **Selling Pre-Trained Models:**
   - **Marketplace Platforms:** List your pre-trained models on AI marketplaces such as TensorFlow Hub, Hugging Face Model Hub, or Algorithmia. These platforms connect model creators with potential buyers.
   - **Direct Sales:** Sell models directly through your website or business platform. Offer models for specific applications, such as image classification or language translation.
2. **Offering Custom AI Solutions:**
   - **Consulting Services:** Provide custom AI model development services to clients. Work with businesses to build tailored models that meet their specific needs.
   - **Contract Projects:** Engage in contract-based projects where you develop AI models based on client specifications and requirements.
3. **Subscription-Based Access:**
   - **API Services:** Develop and offer API access to your AI models. Charge users based on usage, such as the number of API calls or the volume of data processed.
   - **SaaS Platforms:** Create a Software-as-a-Service (SaaS) platform that provides access to your AI models. Offer subscription plans with varying levels of access and features.
4. **Licensing Models:**
   - **Enterprise Licensing:** License your AI models to enterprises for internal use. Negotiate licensing agreements that provide ongoing revenue while allowing companies to integrate and use your models.

- **White-Label Solutions:** Offer white-label versions of your models that other companies can rebrand and integrate into their own products.
5. **Educational and Research Products:**
   - **Training Materials:** Develop educational resources or courses that teach others how to build or use your AI models. Sell these materials through online learning platforms or your own channels.
   - **Research Publications:** Publish research papers or case studies showcasing your AI models. This can enhance your reputation and attract opportunities for model licensing or partnerships.

Marketing and Selling AI Models

Effectively marketing and selling your AI models involves several strategies:

1. **Building a Strong Online Presence:**
   - **Website and Portfolio:** Create a professional website showcasing your AI models, including detailed descriptions, use cases, and performance metrics.
   - **Content Marketing:** Write blog posts, whitepapers, or case studies that highlight the value and capabilities of your models. Share insights and success stories to attract potential buyers.
2. **Networking and Outreach:**
   - **Industry Conferences:** Attend AI and technology conferences to network with potential clients and partners. Presenting your

models or participating in panels can increase visibility.
- o **Social Media and Forums:** Engage with AI communities and forums to build relationships and promote your models. Platforms like LinkedIn, Twitter, and Reddit are valuable for outreach.

3. **Customer Support and Engagement:**
   - o **Provide Support:** Offer robust customer support to assist clients with integrating and using your AI models. Address questions and provide resources to enhance user experience.
   - o **Collect Feedback:** Gather feedback from users to improve your models and services. Use insights to make iterative improvements and respond to market needs.

Ethical and Legal Considerations

When building and selling AI models, consider the following ethical and legal aspects:

- **Data Privacy:** Ensure that data used to train models is handled in compliance with data protection regulations. Respect user privacy and secure sensitive information.
- **Bias and Fairness:** Address potential biases in your AI models to ensure they operate fairly and do not perpetuate discrimination. Regularly review and test models for bias.
- **Intellectual Property:** Protect your AI models through patents, copyrights, or trademarks. Clearly define ownership and usage rights in licensing agreements.

Conclusion

Building and selling AI models presents exciting opportunities for monetizing your expertise and contributing to the evolving landscape of artificial intelligence. By understanding the development process, exploring various monetization strategies, and effectively marketing your models, you can create a successful business around AI solutions.

In the next chapter, we will explore advanced topics in AI entrepreneurship, including scaling your AI business, forming strategic partnerships, and navigating emerging trends in the AI industry.

Chapter 8: AI-Powered Consulting Services

The Evolution of AI Consulting

AI consulting is an emerging field that leverages artificial intelligence to provide specialized advice and solutions to businesses across various industries. AI-powered consulting services help organizations harness the potential of AI technologies to solve complex problems, optimize operations, and drive innovation. This chapter explores how to establish and grow an AI consulting business, offering practical insights into delivering value and generating revenue.

Establishing Your AI Consulting Practice

1. **Define Your Niche and Services:**
   - **Identify Specializations:** Determine your areas of expertise within AI, such as machine learning, data analytics, natural language processing, or computer vision. Specializing in a niche allows you to target specific markets and stand out from competitors.
   - **Service Offerings:** Define the range of services you will provide, including AI strategy development, implementation, optimization, and training. Tailor your offerings to address common business needs and challenges.
2. **Build a Strong Brand:**
   - **Professional Branding:** Develop a professional brand identity, including a business name, logo, and website. Your brand

should reflect your expertise and the value you offer.

- o **Showcase Expertise:** Create a portfolio of successful projects and case studies to demonstrate your capabilities. Highlight specific achievements and the impact of your AI solutions.

3. **Acquire Relevant Skills and Certifications:**
   - o **Continuous Learning:** Stay updated with the latest AI advancements and technologies. Pursue relevant certifications or training programs to enhance your credibility and expertise.
   - o **Industry Knowledge:** Gain a deep understanding of the industries you plan to consult in. This knowledge will help you tailor AI solutions to specific industry needs and challenges.

Delivering AI Consulting Services

1. **Client Engagement:**
   - o **Initial Assessment:** Begin with a thorough assessment of the client's needs, goals, and existing infrastructure. Understand their business processes and identify opportunities where AI can add value.
   - o **Proposal Development:** Develop a detailed proposal outlining your approach, deliverables, timeline, and costs. Clearly communicate the benefits and ROI of your AI solutions.
2. **Solution Design and Implementation:**
   - o **Customized Solutions:** Design AI solutions tailored to the client's specific needs. This may involve developing custom models, integrating

existing tools, or implementing new AI technologies.
- o **Project Management:** Use project management tools and methodologies to ensure timely and efficient implementation. Regularly update clients on progress and address any issues promptly.

3. **Training and Support:**
   - o **Client Training:** Provide training sessions to help clients understand and utilize the AI solutions effectively. Offer resources, documentation, and hands-on training as needed.
   - o **Ongoing Support:** Offer post-implementation support to address any challenges and ensure the AI solutions continue to meet client needs. Provide maintenance and updates as part of your service offering.

Monetizing AI Consulting Services

1. **Consulting Fees:**
   - o **Hourly or Daily Rates:** Charge clients based on the time spent working on their projects. This model is suitable for short-term engagements or advisory services.
   - o **Project-Based Fees:** Offer fixed fees for specific projects or deliverables. Clearly define the scope and objectives to avoid scope creep and ensure clarity in pricing.

2. **Retainer Agreements:**
   - o **Ongoing Support:** Establish retainer agreements where clients pay a regular fee for ongoing consulting services. This model provides stability and allows for long-term client relationships.

- o **Strategic Partnerships:** Develop strategic partnerships with clients for continuous collaboration on AI initiatives. Offer value-added services and insights to strengthen the relationship.

3. **Performance-Based Pricing:**
   - o **Outcome-Based Fees:** Charge fees based on the results and impact of your AI solutions. This approach aligns your compensation with the value delivered to the client.
   - o **Success Metrics:** Define clear success metrics and performance indicators to measure the effectiveness of your solutions. Ensure that both parties agree on the criteria for success.

Scaling Your AI Consulting Business

1. **Expanding Your Team:**
   - o **Hiring Experts:** As your business grows, consider hiring additional consultants or experts with complementary skills. Building a diverse team can enhance your service offerings and capacity.
   - o **Freelancers and Contractors:** Engage freelance or contract professionals for specific projects or expertise. This approach provides flexibility and access to specialized skills.

2. **Developing Proprietary Tools:**
   - o **AI Tools and Platforms:** Invest in developing proprietary AI tools or platforms that can be used across multiple client engagements. This can differentiate your consulting services and offer added value.
   - o **Productized Services:** Create standardized AI solutions or packages that can be offered to

multiple clients. This approach can streamline service delivery and improve scalability.

3. **Marketing and Outreach:**
   - ○ **Thought Leadership:** Establish yourself as a thought leader in the AI consulting space by publishing articles, giving talks, and participating in industry events. Share insights and showcase your expertise.
   - ○ **Networking:** Build a strong network of industry contacts and potential clients. Attend conferences, join professional organizations, and leverage social media to connect with key stakeholders.

Ethical and Legal Considerations

1. **Data Privacy and Security:**
   - ○ **Compliance:** Ensure that your AI consulting practices comply with data protection regulations, such as GDPR or CCPA. Safeguard client data and implement robust security measures.
   - ○ **Ethical Use of AI:** Address ethical considerations in AI, such as bias and fairness. Ensure that your solutions adhere to ethical standards and promote responsible AI practices.

2. **Intellectual Property:**
   - ○ **Ownership Rights:** Clearly define ownership rights and intellectual property terms in consulting agreements. Ensure that both parties understand the rights to AI models, data, and other deliverables.
   - ○ **Non-Disclosure Agreements:** Use non-disclosure agreements (NDAs) to protect

sensitive information and maintain confidentiality during client engagements.

Conclusion

AI-powered consulting services offer significant opportunities to provide value to businesses and generate revenue. By defining your niche, delivering tailored solutions, and implementing effective monetization strategies, you can build a successful consulting practice in the rapidly evolving field of artificial intelligence.

In the next chapter, we will explore advanced topics in scaling your AI business, including forming strategic partnerships, navigating emerging trends, and leveraging new technologies for growth.

Chapter 9: Investing in AI Startups

The Appeal of AI Startups

AI startups are at the forefront of technological innovation, offering unique solutions across various industries. Investing in these startups presents an opportunity to be part of groundbreaking advancements and potentially reap significant financial rewards. This chapter explores the key considerations and strategies for investing in AI startups, helping you navigate this dynamic and high-potential sector.

Understanding the AI Startup Ecosystem

1. **Market Trends and Opportunities:**
   - **Sector Growth:** The AI industry is rapidly expanding, with applications in healthcare, finance, retail, and more. Stay informed about market trends and emerging sectors where AI is making an impact.
   - **Technology Advancements:** Understand the latest advancements in AI technologies, such as machine learning, deep learning, and natural language processing. Identifying promising technologies can guide your investment decisions.
2. **Startup Landscape:**
   - **Types of Startups:** AI startups vary in focus, from developing new algorithms and models to creating AI-driven products and services. Evaluate startups based on their technology stack, business model, and target market.

- o **Funding Stages:** AI startups may be at different funding stages, including seed, early-stage, or growth stage. Each stage presents unique opportunities and risks.

Evaluating AI Startups

1. **Technology and Innovation:**
   - o **Product or Solution:** Assess the startup's AI product or solution. Evaluate its technological novelty, effectiveness, and potential to address real-world problems.
   - o **Competitive Advantage:** Determine the startup's competitive edge. Look for unique technologies, proprietary algorithms, or innovative approaches that differentiate them from competitors.
2. **Market Potential:**
   - o **Target Market:** Analyze the target market for the startup's AI solution. Consider the size of the market, growth potential, and current demand for AI-driven solutions.
   - o **Scalability:** Evaluate the startup's potential for scalability. Consider factors such as market size, business model, and the ability to expand into new regions or applications.
3. **Team and Leadership:**
   - o **Founders and Team:** Assess the startup's leadership team and their expertise in AI and related fields. Strong technical and managerial capabilities are crucial for the success of a startup.
   - o **Advisory Board:** Consider the presence of an advisory board with industry experts and experienced professionals. A strong advisory

board can provide valuable guidance and connections.

4. **Financial Metrics:**
   - **Revenue and Growth:** Review the startup's financial performance, including revenue, profit margins, and growth trajectory. Analyze financial projections and the startup's path to profitability.
   - **Funding History:** Examine the startup's funding history, including previous rounds of investment and current valuation. Assess the terms of previous investments and the involvement of other investors.

Investment Strategies

1. **Direct Investments:**
   - **Equity Stake:** Invest directly in AI startups by purchasing equity shares. This typically involves participating in funding rounds and negotiating terms with the startup's founders.
   - **Convertible Notes:** Consider investing through convertible notes, which are debt instruments that convert into equity at a later stage. This can provide a more flexible investment structure.

2. **Venture Capital Funds:**
   - **VC Firms:** Invest in AI-focused venture capital (VC) funds that specialize in funding AI startups. VC firms provide capital to startups and often offer strategic support and mentorship.
   - **Fund Selection:** Choose VC funds with a strong track record in AI investments and a portfolio of successful startups. Evaluate the

fund's investment strategy and management team.

3. **Angel Investing:**
   - **Early-Stage Investments:** Participate as an angel investor, providing early-stage funding to AI startups. Angel investors often take an active role in mentoring and advising startups.
   - **Investment Networks:** Join angel investing networks or groups that focus on AI startups. These networks provide access to investment opportunities and facilitate connections with other investors.

4. **Crowdfunding Platforms:**
   - **Equity Crowdfunding:** Explore equity crowdfunding platforms that offer investment opportunities in AI startups. Platforms like SeedInvest or Crowdcube allow investors to buy shares in early-stage companies.
   - **Rewards-Based Crowdfunding:** Consider rewards-based crowdfunding platforms for investing in AI startups that offer innovative products or services. Supporters receive early access or other rewards in exchange for their investment.

Mitigating Risks

1. **Due Diligence:**
   - **Thorough Research:** Conduct thorough due diligence before investing. Research the startup's technology, market potential, financials, and team. Seek independent opinions and reviews.
   - **Legal and Compliance:** Ensure that the startup complies with relevant regulations and legal

requirements. Review legal agreements and investment terms carefully.

2. **Diversification:**
   - **Spread Investments:** Diversify your investments across multiple AI startups to mitigate risk. Avoid putting all your capital into a single startup or sector.
   - **Sector and Stage Diversification:** Invest in startups at different stages and within various AI sub-sectors. This approach can balance potential returns and reduce exposure to individual startup failures.

3. **Exit Strategies:**
   - **Planned Exits:** Develop a clear exit strategy for your investments. Consider potential exit scenarios, such as acquisition, IPO, or secondary sales of equity.
   - **Monitoring Performance:** Regularly monitor the performance of your investments and stay informed about the startup's progress. Adjust your exit strategy based on performance and market conditions.

Ethical Considerations

1. **Ethical AI Practices:**
   - **Responsible AI:** Evaluate startups based on their commitment to ethical AI practices. Ensure that their technologies promote fairness, transparency, and accountability.
   - **Impact Assessment:** Consider the social and environmental impact of the startup's AI solutions. Support startups that contribute positively to society and address ethical challenges.

2. **Investment Ethics:**

- ○ **Transparent Practices:** Ensure that investment practices are transparent and align with your values. Avoid startups with questionable business practices or those involved in unethical activities.

Conclusion

Investing in AI startups offers the potential for significant financial returns and the opportunity to support cutting-edge innovations. By understanding the AI startup ecosystem, evaluating startups thoroughly, and employing effective investment strategies, you can make informed decisions and contribute to the advancement of artificial intelligence.

In the next chapter, we will explore advanced strategies for scaling AI ventures, including forming strategic partnerships, navigating emerging trends, and leveraging new technologies for business growth.

Chapter 10: AI in E-commerce and Dropshipping

Transforming E-commerce with AI

Artificial Intelligence is revolutionizing the e-commerce and dropshipping industries by enhancing customer experiences, optimizing operations, and driving sales. AI technologies enable businesses to streamline processes, make data-driven decisions, and personalize interactions at scale. This chapter explores the applications of AI in e-commerce and dropshipping, and how these technologies can be leveraged for success.

AI Applications in E-commerce

1. **Personalized Shopping Experiences:**
   - **Recommendation Systems:** AI algorithms analyze customer behavior and preferences to provide personalized product recommendations. This can increase conversion rates and average order value by suggesting relevant products.
   - **Dynamic Pricing:** AI-powered pricing tools adjust prices in real-time based on demand, competition, and customer behavior. This helps maximize revenue and respond to market changes.
2. **Customer Service and Support:**
   - **Chatbots:** AI-driven chatbots handle customer inquiries, provide instant support, and guide users through the purchasing process. They

enhance customer satisfaction by offering 24/7 assistance.
- o **Sentiment Analysis:** AI tools analyze customer feedback and social media interactions to gauge sentiment and identify areas for improvement. This helps businesses address issues proactively and enhance their offerings.

3. **Inventory Management:**
   - o **Demand Forecasting:** AI models predict product demand based on historical sales data, trends, and external factors. Accurate forecasting helps optimize inventory levels, reduce stockouts, and minimize excess inventory.
   - o **Automated Replenishment:** AI systems automate inventory replenishment by monitoring stock levels and triggering orders when thresholds are met. This ensures that popular products remain in stock and reduces manual oversight.

4. **Fraud Detection and Prevention:**
   - o **Transaction Monitoring:** AI algorithms detect unusual patterns in transactions that may indicate fraudulent activity. By identifying potential fraud early, businesses can protect themselves and their customers.
   - o **Account Security:** AI-driven security measures, such as biometric authentication and behavioral analysis, enhance account security and prevent unauthorized access.

5. **Marketing and Advertising:**
   - o **Targeted Advertising:** AI tools analyze customer data to create targeted advertising campaigns. This includes personalized email marketing, social media ads, and retargeting

efforts that resonate with specific audience segments.

- o **Content Creation:** AI-powered content generation tools assist in creating engaging marketing materials, including product descriptions, blog posts, and social media content.

AI in Dropshipping

1. **Supplier and Product Selection:**
   - o **Supplier Matching:** AI tools analyze supplier data and product reviews to identify reliable suppliers and high-quality products. This helps dropshippers choose the best partners for their businesses.
   - o **Product Trend Analysis:** AI algorithms identify trending products and market demands, helping dropshippers select products that are likely to sell well.
2. **Order Processing and Fulfillment:**
   - o **Automated Order Management:** AI systems streamline order processing by automating tasks such as order confirmation, tracking updates, and customer notifications. This reduces manual work and improves efficiency.
   - o **Logistics Optimization:** AI tools optimize shipping routes and delivery times, ensuring faster and more cost-effective fulfillment. This enhances customer satisfaction and reduces shipping costs.
3. **Customer Insights and Analytics:**
   - o **Behavior Analysis:** AI analyzes customer behavior and purchasing patterns to provide insights into preferences and trends. This data helps dropshippers make informed decisions

about product offerings and marketing
strategies.

- o **Sales Forecasting:** AI models forecast future
  sales based on historical data and market
  trends. This helps dropshippers plan inventory,
  marketing efforts, and resource allocation
  effectively.

4. **Competitive Analysis:**
   - o **Market Research:** AI tools conduct
     competitive analysis by monitoring
     competitors' pricing, promotions, and product
     offerings. This information helps dropshippers
     stay competitive and adjust their strategies
     accordingly.
   - o **Price Optimization:** AI algorithms analyze
     competitor pricing and market conditions to
     recommend optimal pricing strategies. This
     ensures that dropshippers remain competitive
     while maximizing profit margins.

Implementing AI in E-commerce and Dropshipping

1. **Choosing the Right AI Tools:**
   - o **Evaluate Solutions:** Assess various AI tools
     and platforms based on your specific needs,
     such as recommendation engines, chatbots, or
     inventory management systems. Choose tools
     that integrate seamlessly with your existing
     systems.
   - o **Vendor Selection:** Research and select
     reputable AI vendors or service providers.
     Look for providers with a track record of
     successful implementations and strong
     customer support.
2. **Integration and Customization:**

- System Integration: Ensure that AI tools integrate smoothly with your e-commerce platform, CRM, and other systems. Proper integration is essential for maximizing the benefits of AI technologies.
- Customization: Customize AI solutions to fit your business needs and objectives. Tailor recommendation algorithms, chatbots, and marketing tools to align with your brand and customer preferences.

3. **Monitoring and Optimization:**
   - Performance Tracking: Regularly monitor the performance of AI tools and their impact on key metrics such as sales, customer satisfaction, and operational efficiency. Use analytics to identify areas for improvement.
   - Continuous Improvement: Continuously optimize AI models and strategies based on performance data and feedback. Adjust algorithms, update product recommendations, and refine marketing campaigns as needed.

Ethical and Practical Considerations

1. **Data Privacy:**
   - Compliance: Ensure that your use of AI complies with data protection regulations, such as GDPR or CCPA. Safeguard customer data and be transparent about data collection and usage practices.
   - Customer Trust: Build trust with customers by clearly communicating how their data is used and offering options for data control and privacy.

2. **Bias and Fairness:**

- o **Algorithmic Fairness:** Address potential biases in AI algorithms to ensure fair and unbiased outcomes. Regularly review and test AI systems to identify and mitigate biases.
- o **Inclusive Practices:** Ensure that AI-driven recommendations and marketing efforts are inclusive and do not discriminate against specific groups or demographics.

Conclusion

AI technologies are transforming the e-commerce and dropshipping industries by enhancing customer experiences, optimizing operations, and driving growth. By leveraging AI applications effectively, businesses can gain a competitive edge, streamline processes, and deliver personalized experiences that resonate with their customers. As AI continues to evolve, staying informed and adapting to new technologies will be key to achieving long-term success in the dynamic e-commerce landscape.

In the next chapter, we will explore advanced strategies for scaling AI-driven businesses, including forming strategic partnerships, navigating emerging trends, and leveraging new technologies for sustainable growth.

Chapter 11: Automating Business Processes with AI

The Power of Process Automation

Business process automation (BPA) using artificial intelligence (AI) can dramatically enhance efficiency, reduce costs, and improve accuracy. By automating routine tasks and complex workflows, AI helps businesses streamline operations, allowing employees to focus on more strategic activities. This chapter explores how AI can be applied to automate various business processes, the benefits of automation, and best practices for implementation.

Key Areas for AI-Driven Automation

1. **Customer Service Automation:**
    - **Chatbots and Virtual Assistants:** AI-driven chatbots handle customer inquiries, provide support, and resolve issues in real-time. They can manage routine questions, process requests, and escalate complex issues to human agents when necessary.
    - **Automated Ticketing Systems:** AI systems categorize and prioritize customer support tickets, ensuring timely responses and efficient resolution. They can route tickets to the appropriate department or agent based on predefined criteria.
2. **Sales and Marketing Automation:**
    - **Lead Scoring and Nurturing:** AI algorithms analyze customer data to score and prioritize leads based on their likelihood to convert.

Automated systems then engage with leads through personalized emails, content, and follow-ups.

- o **Campaign Management:** AI tools optimize marketing campaigns by analyzing performance data, adjusting targeting strategies, and automating ad placements. This improves ROI and ensures that marketing efforts are aligned with audience preferences.

3. **Human Resources and Recruitment:**
   - o **Resume Screening:** AI-powered systems automate the resume screening process by evaluating candidate qualifications and matching them to job requirements. This reduces the time and effort required to identify suitable candidates.
   - o **Employee Onboarding:** AI streamlines the onboarding process by automating paperwork, training schedules, and initial orientation tasks. This ensures a smoother transition for new hires and improves overall efficiency.

4. **Finance and Accounting:**
   - o **Invoice Processing:** AI systems automate the extraction, validation, and processing of invoices. They can match invoices to purchase orders, detect discrepancies, and facilitate timely payments.
   - o **Expense Management:** AI tools categorize and track expenses, automatically flagging anomalies or policy violations. This reduces manual effort and enhances accuracy in financial reporting.

5. **Supply Chain and Inventory Management:**
   - o **Demand Forecasting:** AI models analyze historical data and market trends to predict demand for products. This helps businesses

optimize inventory levels, reduce stockouts, and minimize excess inventory.
- o **Order Fulfillment:** AI-driven systems automate order processing, including inventory checks, order placement, and shipment tracking. This speeds up fulfillment and reduces errors.

6. **Operations and Workflow Automation:**
   - o **Process Optimization:** AI tools analyze business processes to identify inefficiencies and recommend improvements. They can automate routine tasks, streamline workflows, and enhance overall operational efficiency.
   - o **Predictive Maintenance:** AI systems monitor equipment and machinery performance to predict maintenance needs. This prevents unexpected breakdowns and reduces downtime through proactive maintenance scheduling.

Benefits of AI-Driven Automation

1. **Increased Efficiency:**
   - o **Time Savings:** Automation reduces the time spent on repetitive tasks, allowing employees to focus on higher-value activities. This accelerates workflows and boosts overall productivity.
   - o **Operational Speed:** AI-driven processes operate at a faster pace than manual methods, leading to quicker decision-making and execution.

2. **Cost Reduction:**
   - o **Labor Costs:** By automating routine tasks, businesses can reduce labor costs and reallocate resources to strategic areas. This lowers overall operational expenses.

- Error Reduction: AI minimizes human errors, reducing the costs associated with correcting mistakes and improving accuracy in process execution.

3. **Enhanced Accuracy and Consistency:**
   - **Data Precision:** AI algorithms provide consistent and accurate data analysis, leading to reliable insights and decision-making. This ensures that processes are executed with precision.
   - **Standardized Processes:** Automation enforces standardized procedures, reducing variability and ensuring consistent outcomes across different operations.

4. **Scalability:**
   - **Growth Adaptation:** AI-driven automation scales easily with business growth. As transaction volumes and operational demands increase, automated systems can handle larger workloads without additional manual effort.
   - **Flexibility:** Automated systems can be adapted to new processes and requirements, allowing businesses to remain agile and responsive to changing needs.

Implementing AI-Driven Automation

1. **Identifying Automation Opportunities:**
   - **Process Assessment:** Conduct an assessment of existing business processes to identify tasks and workflows that can benefit from automation. Focus on high-volume, repetitive, and time-consuming tasks.
   - **Prioritization:** Prioritize automation opportunities based on potential impact, ease of implementation, and alignment with business

goals. Start with processes that offer the greatest potential for improvement.

2. **Selecting the Right AI Tools:**
   - **Tool Evaluation:** Evaluate AI tools and platforms based on their capabilities, ease of integration, and compatibility with existing systems. Choose tools that address specific automation needs and offer scalability.
   - **Vendor Selection:** Research and select reputable AI vendors with a track record of successful implementations. Consider factors such as customer support, product updates, and user reviews.

3. **Integration and Customization:**
   - **System Integration:** Ensure that AI tools integrate seamlessly with existing systems and workflows. Proper integration is essential for achieving the desired automation outcomes and maintaining operational continuity.
   - **Customization:** Customize AI solutions to fit the specific requirements and processes of your business. Tailor algorithms, workflows, and interfaces to align with organizational needs.

4. **Monitoring and Optimization:**
   - **Performance Tracking:** Monitor the performance of automated processes and assess their impact on key metrics such as efficiency, accuracy, and cost. Use analytics to identify areas for improvement.
   - **Continuous Improvement:** Continuously optimize AI-driven automation based on performance data and feedback. Adjust algorithms, update workflows, and refine processes to enhance outcomes.

Ethical and Practical Considerations

1. **Transparency and Accountability:**
   - **Decision-Making Transparency:** Ensure that automated decisions are transparent and explainable. Provide insights into how AI algorithms make decisions and the factors considered.
   - **Accountability:** Establish clear lines of accountability for automated processes. Define roles and responsibilities for overseeing and managing AI-driven automation.
2. **Data Privacy and Security:**
   - **Compliance:** Ensure that automation practices comply with data protection regulations, such as GDPR or CCPA. Implement robust security measures to protect sensitive data.
   - **Data Management:** Regularly review data management practices and address any potential risks related to data privacy and security.

Conclusion

AI-driven automation offers significant benefits for businesses, including increased efficiency, cost reduction, and enhanced accuracy. By identifying automation opportunities, selecting the right tools, and implementing best practices, organizations can streamline operations, improve productivity, and drive growth. As AI technology continues to evolve, staying informed and adapting to new advancements will be key to maximizing the potential of automation.

In the next chapter, we will explore advanced strategies for leveraging AI for innovation, including developing new products, exploring emerging technologies, and staying ahead of industry trends.

Chapter 12: AI in Financial Trading and Investment

The Role of AI in Financial Markets

Artificial Intelligence (AI) is transforming financial trading and investment by offering sophisticated tools for analysis, prediction, and decision-making. AI technologies enhance trading strategies, manage risk, and optimize investment portfolios, making them essential for modern financial operations. This chapter explores how AI is applied in financial trading and investment, its benefits, and best practices for leveraging these technologies.

AI Applications in Financial Trading

1. **Algorithmic Trading:**
   - **High-Frequency Trading (HFT):** AI algorithms execute large volumes of trades at high speeds, capitalizing on small price movements. HFT strategies rely on advanced algorithms and data analytics to make rapid trading decisions.
   - **Automated Trading Systems:** AI-driven trading systems use historical data and predictive models to execute trades based on predefined criteria. These systems can adjust strategies in real-time based on market conditions.
2. **Predictive Analytics:**

- o **Market Forecasting:** AI models analyze historical market data, economic indicators, and news sentiment to forecast future market trends. This helps traders anticipate price movements and make informed decisions.
- o **Price Prediction Models:** Machine learning algorithms predict asset prices by identifying patterns and correlations in historical data. These models can enhance trading strategies and improve accuracy in price forecasts.

3. **Sentiment Analysis:**
   - o **News and Social Media Monitoring:** AI tools analyze news articles, social media posts, and other sources to gauge market sentiment. By understanding investor sentiment, traders can predict market reactions and adjust strategies accordingly.
   - o **Event Impact Analysis:** AI assesses the potential impact of news events, earnings reports, and other market-moving factors. This helps traders evaluate how specific events might affect asset prices and market conditions.

4. **Risk Management:**
   - o **Portfolio Optimization:** AI algorithms optimize investment portfolios by balancing risk and return based on historical performance, market conditions, and investor preferences. This helps in creating diversified and efficient portfolios.
   - o **Risk Assessment:** AI tools evaluate risk factors and detect anomalies in trading patterns. They can identify potential risks, such as market volatility or liquidity issues, and suggest mitigation strategies.

AI Applications in Investment Management

1. **Robo-Advisors:**
   - **Automated Investment Advice:** Robo-advisors use AI algorithms to provide personalized investment advice and portfolio management based on investor profiles and goals. They offer cost-effective solutions for wealth management.
   - **Portfolio Rebalancing:** AI-driven robo-advisors automatically rebalance investment portfolios to maintain desired asset allocations. This ensures that portfolios remain aligned with investment objectives and risk tolerance.
2. **Investment Research:**
   - **Data Analysis:** AI tools analyze vast amounts of financial data, including company reports, market trends, and economic indicators. This provides investors with actionable insights and supports informed decision-making.
   - **Pattern Recognition:** Machine learning algorithms identify patterns and trends in financial data that may not be apparent through traditional analysis. This helps investors uncover hidden opportunities and potential risks.
3. **Fraud Detection:**
   - **Anomaly Detection:** AI systems monitor transactions and investment activities for unusual patterns that may indicate fraudulent behavior. Early detection of anomalies helps prevent financial losses and protect investor assets.
   - **Compliance Monitoring:** AI tools ensure compliance with regulatory requirements by analyzing trading activities and investment practices. They can identify potential violations and alert compliance officers.

4. **Behavioral Finance:**
   - o **Investor Behavior Analysis:** AI analyzes investor behavior to understand decision-making biases and patterns. This helps in designing strategies that account for behavioral tendencies and improve investment outcomes.
   - o **Personalized Investment Strategies:** AI provides tailored investment strategies based on individual investor preferences, risk tolerance, and financial goals. This enhances the relevance and effectiveness of investment advice.

Implementing AI in Financial Trading and Investment

1. **Choosing AI Tools and Platforms:**
   - o **Tool Evaluation:** Assess various AI tools and platforms based on their capabilities, integration options, and suitability for your trading or investment needs. Look for tools that offer robust analytics, predictive modeling, and automation features.
   - o **Vendor Selection:** Select reputable AI vendors with a proven track record in financial trading and investment. Consider factors such as customer support, product updates, and compliance with industry standards.
2. **Integration and Customization:**
   - o **System Integration:** Ensure that AI tools integrate seamlessly with existing trading platforms, data sources, and investment management systems. Proper integration is essential for effective utilization and data consistency.
   - o **Customization:** Customize AI models and algorithms to align with your specific trading

strategies or investment objectives. Tailor predictive models, risk management tools, and portfolio optimization techniques to fit your needs.

3. **Monitoring and Evaluation:**
    o **Performance Tracking:** Regularly monitor the performance of AI-driven trading systems and investment strategies. Evaluate key metrics such as return on investment (ROI), risk-adjusted returns, and system accuracy.
    o **Continuous Improvement:** Continuously refine AI models and strategies based on performance data and market changes. Adjust algorithms, update data sources, and incorporate new insights to enhance effectiveness.

Ethical and Practical Considerations

1. **Data Privacy and Security:**
    o **Compliance:** Ensure that AI-driven trading and investment practices comply with data protection regulations, such as GDPR or CCPA. Implement robust security measures to protect sensitive financial data.
    o **Data Management:** Regularly review data management practices and address any potential risks related to data privacy and security. Safeguard customer information and ensure transparency in data usage.

2. **Algorithmic Bias:**
    o **Bias Mitigation:** Address potential biases in AI algorithms that may impact trading decisions or investment recommendations. Regularly test and validate models to ensure fairness and accuracy.

- o **Transparency:** Ensure transparency in AI decision-making processes. Provide explanations for algorithmic decisions and ensure that stakeholders understand how decisions are made.

Conclusion

AI is reshaping financial trading and investment by offering advanced tools for analysis, prediction, and automation. By leveraging AI technologies, traders and investors can enhance their strategies, manage risks, and optimize portfolios. Implementing AI effectively requires careful selection of tools, integration with existing systems, and continuous monitoring. As AI continues to advance, staying informed and adapting to new developments will be crucial for achieving success in the evolving financial landscape.

In the next chapter, we will explore advanced strategies for leveraging AI for innovation, including developing new products, exploring emerging technologies, and staying ahead of industry trends.

Chapter 13: AI and Real Estate

Transforming Real Estate with AI

Artificial Intelligence (AI) is revolutionizing the real estate industry by enhancing property management, improving investment strategies, and streamlining transactions. AI technologies offer powerful tools for analyzing market trends, predicting property values, and optimizing real estate operations. This chapter explores the various applications of AI in real estate, the benefits of these technologies, and best practices for leveraging AI in the industry.

AI Applications in Real Estate

1. **Property Valuation and Market Analysis:**
   - **Automated Valuation Models (AVMs):** AI-driven AVMs use historical data, market trends, and property characteristics to estimate property values. These models provide accurate and timely valuations, aiding buyers, sellers, and appraisers.
   - **Market Trend Analysis:** AI tools analyze market data, including transaction histories, demographic trends, and economic indicators, to identify emerging trends and forecast future market conditions. This helps investors and real estate professionals make informed decisions.
2. **Lead Generation and Customer Relationship Management:**
   - **Predictive Lead Scoring:** AI algorithms assess and score leads based on their likelihood to

convert. This prioritizes high-potential leads and enhances targeting strategies for real estate agents and brokers.

- o **Personalized Marketing:** AI-powered systems analyze customer behavior and preferences to create personalized marketing campaigns. This includes targeted emails, social media ads, and property recommendations tailored to individual interests.

3. **Property Management and Operations:**
   - o **Smart Building Management:** AI systems optimize building operations by monitoring energy usage, controlling lighting and HVAC systems, and managing maintenance requests. This improves efficiency, reduces costs, and enhances tenant satisfaction.
   - o **Predictive Maintenance:** AI tools predict equipment failures and maintenance needs by analyzing historical data and sensor inputs. This enables proactive maintenance, reducing downtime and extending the lifespan of property assets.

4. **Real Estate Investment and Portfolio Management:**
   - o **Investment Analysis:** AI algorithms evaluate investment opportunities by analyzing property data, market trends, and financial metrics. This helps investors identify high-performing properties and optimize their investment strategies.
   - o **Portfolio Optimization:** AI-driven systems manage and optimize real estate portfolios by analyzing performance metrics, risk factors, and market conditions. This ensures that portfolios are well-balanced and aligned with investment goals.

5. **Tenant Screening and Lease Management:**

- o **Automated Tenant Screening:** AI tools assess rental applications by analyzing credit scores, employment history, and rental history. This streamlines the screening process and reduces the risk of renting to unreliable tenants.
- o **Lease Management:** AI systems automate lease management tasks, including lease renewals, rent collection, and compliance monitoring. This simplifies administrative processes and enhances operational efficiency.

6. **Virtual Tours and Property Visualization:**
   - o **Virtual Reality (VR) and Augmented Reality (AR):** AI-powered VR and AR technologies create immersive property tours and visualizations. This allows potential buyers and tenants to explore properties remotely and visualize potential changes.
   - o **3D Property Modeling:** AI tools generate detailed 3D models of properties, providing realistic representations of spaces and layouts. This aids in marketing, design planning, and decision-making.

Benefits of AI in Real Estate

1. **Increased Efficiency:**
   - o **Time Savings:** AI automates repetitive tasks, such as property valuation, lead generation, and lease management, saving time and reducing manual effort. This allows real estate professionals to focus on higher-value activities.
   - o **Operational Efficiency:** AI optimizes building management and maintenance processes, improving overall operational efficiency and

reducing costs associated with property management.

2. **Enhanced Decision-Making:**
   - o **Data-Driven Insights:** AI provides valuable insights through data analysis and predictive modeling, enabling informed decision-making. This includes accurate property valuations, market forecasts, and investment recommendations.
   - o **Personalization:** AI enhances customer interactions by providing personalized recommendations and marketing strategies, leading to improved customer satisfaction and engagement.

3. **Improved Accuracy:**
   - o **Valuation Precision:** AI-driven AVMs and predictive models offer precise property valuations, reducing errors and discrepancies in property assessments.
   - o **Risk Mitigation:** AI tools identify potential risks and anomalies, helping investors and property managers mitigate risks and make data-driven decisions.

4. **Cost Reduction:**
   - o **Operational Costs:** AI reduces operational costs by automating administrative tasks, optimizing building management, and minimizing maintenance expenses.
   - o **Marketing Costs:** AI-powered marketing tools enhance targeting and personalization, leading to more cost-effective marketing campaigns and higher conversion rates.

Implementing AI in Real Estate

1. **Selecting the Right AI Tools:**

- o **Tool Evaluation:** Evaluate AI tools and platforms based on their features, integration capabilities, and suitability for your real estate operations. Look for tools that address specific needs such as valuation, lead generation, or property management.
- o **Vendor Selection:** Choose reputable AI vendors with a proven track record in the real estate industry. Consider factors such as customer support, product updates, and industry expertise.

2. **Integration and Customization:**
   - o **System Integration:** Ensure that AI tools integrate seamlessly with existing real estate platforms, CRM systems, and data sources. Proper integration is crucial for achieving effective automation and data consistency.
   - o **Customization:** Customize AI solutions to fit the specific requirements and workflows of your real estate business. Tailor algorithms, models, and interfaces to align with your operational needs and goals.

3. **Monitoring and Optimization:**
   - o **Performance Tracking:** Monitor the performance of AI-driven tools and assess their impact on key metrics such as property valuations, lead conversion rates, and operational efficiency. Use analytics to identify areas for improvement.
   - o **Continuous Improvement:** Continuously refine AI models and strategies based on performance data and feedback. Adjust algorithms, update data sources, and incorporate new insights to enhance effectiveness.

Ethical and Practical Considerations

1. **Data Privacy and Security:**
   - **Compliance:** Ensure that AI-driven real estate practices comply with data protection regulations, such as GDPR or CCPA. Implement robust security measures to protect sensitive customer and property data.
   - **Data Management:** Regularly review data management practices and address any potential risks related to data privacy and security. Safeguard customer information and ensure transparency in data usage.
2. **Bias and Fairness:**
   - **Algorithmic Bias:** Address potential biases in AI algorithms that may affect property valuations, tenant screening, or investment recommendations. Regularly test and validate models to ensure fairness and accuracy.
   - **Transparency:** Ensure transparency in AI decision-making processes. Provide clear explanations for algorithmic decisions and ensure that stakeholders understand how decisions are made.

Conclusion

AI is transforming the real estate industry by enhancing property management, improving investment strategies, and streamlining transactions. By leveraging AI technologies effectively, real estate professionals can increase efficiency, enhance decision-making, and reduce costs. Implementing AI requires careful selection of tools, integration with existing systems, and continuous monitoring. As AI continues to evolve, staying informed and adapting to new advancements will be key to achieving success in the dynamic real estate market.

In the next chapter, we will explore advanced strategies for leveraging AI for innovation, including developing new products, exploring emerging technologies, and staying ahead of industry trends.

Chapter 14: Ethical Considerations and Challenges

The Ethical Landscape of AI

As artificial intelligence (AI) becomes increasingly integrated into various aspects of our lives, addressing the ethical considerations and challenges associated with its use is crucial. AI holds tremendous potential for innovation and efficiency, but it also raises important ethical questions related to privacy, fairness, accountability, and transparency. This chapter explores the key ethical issues surrounding AI, the challenges faced by organizations, and best practices for ensuring responsible AI development and deployment.

Key Ethical Considerations

1. **Privacy and Data Protection:**
   - **Data Collection and Usage:** AI systems rely on large datasets to function effectively, often involving sensitive personal information. Ensuring that data is collected, stored, and used in compliance with privacy laws (e.g., GDPR, CCPA) is essential. Organizations must obtain informed consent and provide transparency about data usage.
   - **Data Security:** Protecting data from breaches and unauthorized access is critical. Implementing robust security measures, such as encryption and access controls, helps safeguard sensitive information and maintain user trust.
2. **Bias and Fairness:**

- **Algorithmic Bias:** AI algorithms can perpetuate or even exacerbate existing biases present in training data. Bias in AI can lead to unfair treatment and discrimination, particularly in sensitive areas such as hiring, lending, and law enforcement. Identifying and mitigating biases through diverse data sources and regular audits is crucial.
- **Equity in Outcomes:** Ensuring that AI systems provide equitable outcomes for all users, regardless of race, gender, or socioeconomic status, is a key ethical concern. Fairness in AI involves designing algorithms that promote inclusivity and avoid discriminatory practices.

3. **Transparency and Accountability:**
   - **Explainability:** AI systems can be complex and opaque, making it difficult for users to understand how decisions are made. Promoting transparency and developing explainable AI models help users comprehend the reasoning behind automated decisions.
   - **Responsibility:** Assigning accountability for AI-driven decisions is essential. Organizations must establish clear lines of responsibility for the development, deployment, and oversight of AI systems, ensuring that decisions can be traced back to accountable individuals or teams.

4. **Autonomy and Control:**
   - **Human Oversight:** Maintaining human oversight over AI systems is vital to ensure that automated decisions align with ethical standards and human values. Organizations should implement mechanisms for human intervention and review in critical decision-making processes.

- o **Informed Consent:** Users should be informed about the use of AI in applications that affect them. Providing clear explanations about how AI is used and obtaining explicit consent helps maintain trust and respect for user autonomy.

Challenges in Ethical AI Development

1. **Data Quality and Integrity:**
   - o **Bias in Data:** Poor-quality or biased data can lead to inaccurate and unfair AI outcomes. Ensuring data quality involves sourcing diverse and representative datasets, cleaning and preprocessing data, and regularly updating datasets to reflect current conditions.
   - o **Data Management:** Managing and maintaining data integrity is challenging, particularly when dealing with large volumes of information. Implementing robust data governance practices helps ensure that data remains accurate and reliable.
2. **Regulatory and Compliance Issues:**
   - o **Evolving Regulations:** The regulatory landscape for AI is rapidly evolving, with new laws and guidelines emerging to address ethical concerns. Staying compliant with existing regulations and adapting to new ones requires ongoing monitoring and flexibility.
   - o **Global Standards:** Different regions may have varying standards and regulations regarding AI ethics. Organizations operating globally must navigate these differences and ensure compliance with regional laws and ethical guidelines.
3. **Ethical Design and Development:**

- Ethics in Design: Incorporating ethical considerations into AI design and development processes is essential. This involves adopting ethical guidelines, conducting impact assessments, and involving diverse stakeholders in the design phase.
- Training and Awareness: Ensuring that AI developers and practitioners are trained in ethical principles and aware of potential biases is crucial for responsible AI development. Continuous education and awareness programs help promote ethical practices.

4. Public Perception and Trust:
   - Building Trust: Gaining and maintaining public trust in AI systems is a challenge, particularly when addressing concerns about privacy, bias, and accountability. Transparent communication and ethical practices help build and sustain trust with users and stakeholders.
   - Public Engagement: Engaging with the public and incorporating their feedback into AI development helps address societal concerns and ensures that AI technologies align with public values and expectations.

Best Practices for Ethical AI

1. **Establish Ethical Guidelines:**
   - Develop a Code of Ethics: Create and implement a code of ethics for AI development that outlines principles and standards for responsible AI practices. Ensure that these guidelines address key ethical concerns and are integrated into organizational policies.
   - Ethics Committees: Form ethics committees or advisory boards to oversee AI projects and

provide guidance on ethical issues. These committees can review AI systems, assess potential risks, and recommend improvements.

2. **Promote Transparency and Explainability:**
   - **Explainable AI:** Develop and use explainable AI models that provide clear and understandable explanations for automated decisions. This helps users and stakeholders grasp how AI systems operate and make informed decisions.
   - **Open Communication:** Maintain open communication with users regarding the use of AI, including its benefits, limitations, and potential risks. Transparency fosters trust and helps manage expectations.

3. **Implement Fairness and Bias Mitigation Strategies:**
   - **Bias Audits:** Conduct regular audits of AI systems to identify and address biases. Use diverse datasets, implement fairness algorithms, and involve diverse teams in the development process to promote fairness.
   - **Inclusive Design:** Design AI systems with inclusivity in mind, ensuring that they cater to diverse user groups and avoid discriminatory practices.

4. **Ensure Compliance and Accountability:**
   - **Compliance Monitoring:** Regularly monitor compliance with data protection regulations, ethical guidelines, and industry standards. Implement processes for auditing and reporting compliance.
   - **Accountability Mechanisms:** Establish mechanisms for holding individuals and teams accountable for AI-driven decisions. Ensure that responsibilities are clearly defined and that oversight is maintained.

Conclusion

Ethical considerations and challenges in AI development require careful attention and proactive management. By addressing issues related to privacy, bias, transparency, and accountability, organizations can develop and deploy AI technologies responsibly. Implementing best practices, engaging with stakeholders, and staying informed about evolving regulations are essential for ensuring that AI serves the greater good and aligns with ethical standards. As AI continues to advance, maintaining a focus on ethical principles will be key to fostering trust and achieving positive outcomes in the ever-evolving landscape of artificial intelligence.

In the next chapter, we will explore advanced strategies for leveraging AI for innovation, including developing new products, exploring emerging technologies, and staying ahead of industry trends.

Chapter 15: Future Trends and Opportunities in AI

Emerging Trends in AI

As artificial intelligence (AI) continues to evolve, several emerging trends are shaping its future and creating new opportunities across various industries. Staying ahead of these trends is crucial for leveraging AI's potential and addressing upcoming challenges. This chapter explores key trends and opportunities in AI, offering insights into what the future may hold.

1. Advanced AI and Machine Learning Techniques

1. **Generative AI:**
   - **Creative Applications:** Generative AI models, such as Generative Adversarial Networks (GANs) and diffusion models, are revolutionizing creative fields by generating realistic images, videos, and text. These models have applications in art, design, and media production.
   - **Synthetic Data:** Generative AI is also used to create synthetic data for training other AI models, addressing data scarcity and privacy concerns. This synthetic data can simulate various scenarios and enhance model robustness.
2. **Explainable AI (XAI):**
   - **Transparency:** As AI systems become more complex, explainable AI techniques aim to make AI decision-making processes more

transparent and interpretable. XAI helps users understand how AI models arrive at their conclusions, promoting trust and accountability.
- o **Regulatory Compliance:** XAI is increasingly important for compliance with regulations that require transparency in AI decision-making. It provides insights into model behavior and supports fair and ethical AI practices.

3. **Autonomous Systems:**
- o **Self-Driving Vehicles:** Advances in autonomous driving technology are transforming transportation. AI-driven self-driving cars, trucks, and drones promise increased safety, efficiency, and convenience in transportation and logistics.
- o **Robotic Automation:** AI-powered robots are becoming more capable of performing complex tasks in various industries, including manufacturing, healthcare, and agriculture. Autonomous robots can enhance productivity and reduce labor costs.

2. AI in Emerging Technologies

1. **Quantum Computing:**
- o **Accelerated AI Processing:** Quantum computing holds the potential to revolutionize AI by significantly accelerating data processing and solving complex problems beyond the capabilities of classical computers. Quantum algorithms could lead to breakthroughs in machine learning and optimization.
- o **Enhanced AI Models:** Quantum computing may enable the development of more advanced AI models that can handle larger datasets,

perform more intricate computations, and achieve higher accuracy in predictions.

2. **Edge AI:**
   - **Decentralized Processing:** Edge AI involves processing data on local devices, such as smartphones, IoT sensors, and edge servers, rather than relying on centralized cloud computing. This reduces latency, enhances privacy, and improves real-time decision-making.
   - **IoT Integration:** Edge AI enables smarter IoT devices that can analyze data and make decisions locally. This has applications in smart homes, industrial automation, and healthcare, where real-time data processing is crucial.

3. **AI and 5G Technology:**
   - **Enhanced Connectivity:** The rollout of 5G technology provides faster and more reliable connectivity, supporting the deployment of AI applications that require high-speed data transfer and low latency. This includes real-time analytics, augmented reality (AR), and virtual reality (VR).
   - **IoT Expansion:** 5G enhances the capabilities of IoT devices, enabling more sophisticated AI-driven applications in areas such as smart cities, connected vehicles, and industrial IoT.

3. Opportunities in AI-Driven Innovation

1. **Personalized Experiences:**
   - **Tailored Recommendations:** AI enables highly personalized experiences in various sectors, such as retail, entertainment, and healthcare. By analyzing user preferences and

behavior, AI can deliver customized recommendations, content, and services.
- o **Adaptive Learning:** In education, AI-driven adaptive learning platforms provide personalized learning experiences based on individual student needs and progress. This enhances educational outcomes and supports diverse learning styles.

2. **Healthcare Advancements:**
- o **Precision Medicine:** AI is advancing precision medicine by analyzing genetic data, patient records, and clinical research to develop personalized treatment plans and drug therapies. This improves patient outcomes and reduces trial-and-error in treatment.
- o **Early Diagnosis and Prevention:** AI-powered diagnostic tools assist in early detection of diseases, such as cancer and cardiovascular conditions, by analyzing medical imaging, biomarkers, and patient data. This leads to earlier interventions and better healthcare outcomes.

3. **Sustainable Solutions:**
- o **Environmental Monitoring:** AI is used to monitor and analyze environmental data, such as air quality, deforestation, and climate change. AI-driven solutions help in developing sustainable practices and addressing environmental challenges.
- o **Energy Optimization:** AI technologies optimize energy consumption in various industries, including smart grids, renewable energy systems, and energy-efficient buildings. This contributes to reducing carbon footprints and promoting sustainability.

4. Addressing Future Challenges

1. **Ethical and Regulatory Frameworks:**
   - **Developing Standards:** As AI technologies evolve, establishing ethical guidelines and regulatory frameworks is essential to address issues related to privacy, fairness, and accountability. Collaborative efforts among governments, organizations, and researchers will shape the future of AI governance.
   - **Global Cooperation:** International cooperation is needed to develop and implement global standards for AI ethics and regulation. Addressing ethical concerns on a global scale ensures that AI benefits are equitably distributed and potential risks are managed effectively.
2. **Workforce Implications:**
   - **Reskilling and Upskilling:** The rise of AI and automation will impact the workforce, requiring reskilling and upskilling to adapt to new job roles and technological advancements. Investing in education and training programs will help individuals navigate the evolving job market.
   - **Job Creation and Transformation:** While AI may lead to job displacement in some sectors, it also creates new opportunities in areas such as AI development, data science, and AI ethics. Embracing these changes will foster innovation and economic growth.

Conclusion

The future of AI is marked by rapid advancements, emerging technologies, and significant opportunities for innovation across various industries. By staying informed about emerging trends and addressing potential challenges, organizations and individuals can harness the full potential of AI while ensuring responsible and ethical use. Embracing these future trends will pave the way for transformative solutions and drive progress in the evolving landscape of artificial intelligence.

In the final chapter, we will summarize the key takeaways from the book and provide actionable insights for leveraging AI to achieve personal and professional success.

Chapter 16: Conclusion and Action Plan

Summarizing the Journey

As we reach the end of this exploration into the world of artificial intelligence (AI) and its potential for transforming lives and businesses, it's crucial to reflect on the key insights and actionable strategies discussed throughout the book. From understanding the fundamentals of AI to delving into various avenues for monetization and addressing ethical considerations, we've covered a broad spectrum of AI applications and opportunities. This concluding chapter synthesizes these insights and provides a practical action plan to help you leverage AI effectively.

Key Takeaways

1. **Understanding AI:**
   - AI is a rapidly evolving field with applications across diverse industries. A solid understanding of its technologies, from machine learning to natural language processing, is foundational for harnessing its potential.
2. **Monetizing AI:**
   - There are numerous ways to monetize AI, including freelancing with AI skills, creating AI-driven products, and offering AI-powered consulting services. Identifying and pursuing these opportunities can lead to significant financial and professional rewards.
3. **Ethical Considerations:**

- Responsible AI development involves addressing privacy, bias, transparency, and accountability. Adhering to ethical practices ensures that AI technologies are used fairly and benefit society as a whole.

4. **Future Trends:**
   - Staying abreast of emerging trends such as generative AI, edge computing, and quantum computing can position you at the forefront of innovation and open new avenues for growth and success.

Action Plan for Leveraging AI

1. **Define Your Objectives:**
   - **Identify Goals:** Determine what you aim to achieve with AI, whether it's starting a new business, enhancing current operations, or exploring new career opportunities. Clearly defined goals will guide your strategy and actions.
   - **Assess Needs:** Evaluate the specific AI technologies and solutions that align with your objectives. Understand the requirements and resources needed to implement these technologies effectively.
2. **Acquire and Develop Skills:**
   - **Educational Resources:** Invest in learning opportunities such as online courses, certifications, and workshops to build a solid foundation in AI. Focus on areas relevant to your goals, whether it's machine learning, data analysis, or AI ethics.
   - **Hands-On Experience:** Gain practical experience by working on AI projects, participating in hackathons, or contributing to

open-source AI initiatives. Practical experience enhances your understanding and capabilities.

3. **Explore Monetization Strategies:**
   o **Freelancing and Consulting:** Offer AI-related services on freelancing platforms or as a consultant. Build a portfolio showcasing your expertise and success stories to attract potential clients.
   o **Product Development:** Develop and market AI-driven products or digital tools. Validate your ideas through market research and pilot testing to ensure they meet user needs and preferences.

4. **Address Ethical and Practical Challenges:**
   o **Implement Best Practices:** Follow ethical guidelines and best practices for AI development and deployment. Ensure compliance with data protection regulations and implement fairness and transparency measures.
   o **Monitor and Adapt:** Continuously monitor the impact of your AI initiatives and adapt your strategies based on feedback and evolving trends. Stay informed about regulatory changes and technological advancements.

5. **Stay Informed and Innovative:**
   o **Follow Industry Trends:** Keep up with the latest developments in AI through industry news, research papers, and professional networks. Engaging with the AI community helps you stay ahead of emerging trends and opportunities.
   o **Foster Innovation:** Embrace a mindset of innovation and experimentation. Explore new AI technologies and applications, and be open

to iterative improvements and creative solutions.

Conclusion

The journey through the world of AI reveals its immense potential to transform industries, drive innovation, and create new opportunities. By understanding the fundamentals, exploring various monetization avenues, and addressing ethical considerations, you can harness the power of AI to achieve your goals and make a meaningful impact.

As you move forward, remember that AI is not just a technological advancement but a transformative force that can enhance personal and professional endeavors. Embrace the opportunities, navigate the challenges with responsibility, and stay committed to continuous learning and adaptation.

With a clear action plan and a strategic approach, you are well-equipped to leverage AI's potential and shape a successful future in this dynamic field. The possibilities are boundless, and the future is bright for those who are prepared to lead and innovate with AI.

Glossary

AI (Artificial Intelligence): The field of computer science dedicated to creating systems that can perform tasks that typically require human intelligence, such as learning, reasoning, and problem-solving.

Algorithm: A set of rules or procedures for solving a problem or performing a task, often implemented in software to process data and make decisions.

Bias: Systematic error or unfairness in AI models that can arise from biased data, leading to discriminatory outcomes or inaccurate predictions.

Deep Learning: A subset of machine learning that uses neural networks with multiple layers (deep networks) to model complex patterns and relationships in data.

Generative AI: AI technologies that create new content or data, such as images, text, or music, based on learned patterns from existing data. Examples include Generative Adversarial Networks (GANs) and diffusion models.

Machine Learning (ML): A subset of AI focused on developing algorithms that enable computers to learn from and make predictions or decisions based on data without being explicitly programmed.

Natural Language Processing (NLP): A field of AI concerned with the interaction between computers and human language, enabling machines to understand, interpret, and generate human language.

Neural Networks: Computational models inspired by the human brain, consisting of interconnected nodes (neurons) that process information and learn patterns from data.

Quantum Computing: A type of computing that leverages the principles of quantum mechanics to perform computations much faster than classical computers for certain types of problems.

Robotics: The branch of AI that involves the design and creation of robots, which are machines capable of carrying out tasks autonomously or semi-autonomously.

Synthetic Data: Data generated by AI models rather than collected from real-world sources. It is used to train other AI models, especially when real data is scarce or sensitive.

Transparency: The degree to which the inner workings and decision-making processes of an AI system are visible and understandable to users and stakeholders.

XAI (Explainable AI): AI methods and techniques aimed at making the outputs of AI models interpretable and understandable to humans, addressing the "black-box" nature of complex models.

Additional Resources

Books and Articles:

1. **"Artificial Intelligence: A Modern Approach"** by Stuart Russell and Peter Norvig
   - A comprehensive textbook covering the fundamental concepts and techniques in AI.
2. **"Deep Learning"** by Ian Goodfellow, Yoshua Bengio, and Aaron Courville
   - An in-depth exploration of deep learning techniques and their applications.
3. **"The Age of Em: Work, Love, and Life when Robots Rule the Earth"** by Robin Hanson
   - A thought-provoking book on the future of AI and its potential impact on society.
4. **"Weapons of Math Destruction: How Big Data Increases Inequality and Threatens Democracy"** by Cathy O'Neil
   - An examination of the ethical implications and societal impacts of big data and AI.
5. **"AI Superpowers: China, Silicon Valley, and the New World Order"** by Kai-Fu Lee
   - Insights into the global AI landscape and the competition between major tech hubs.

Online Courses and Certifications:

1. **Coursera – "Machine Learning" by Andrew Ng**
   - A foundational course on machine learning concepts and algorithms.

2. **edX – "Artificial Intelligence MicroMasters Program" by Columbia University**
   - A series of advanced courses covering various aspects of AI.
3. **Udacity – "AI for Everyone" by Andrew Ng**
   - A course designed to provide a broad understanding of AI concepts and applications.
4. **DataCamp – "Introduction to Python for Data Science"**
   - A practical course for learning Python programming with a focus on data science and AI.
5. **Kaggle – "Intro to Machine Learning"**
   - A beginner-friendly course on machine learning techniques and their implementation using Python.

Professional Organizations and Networks:

1. **Association for the Advancement of Artificial Intelligence (AAAI)**
   - A leading organization dedicated to promoting research and development in AI.
2. **Institute of Electrical and Electronics Engineers (IEEE) – AI and Robotics Technical Community**
   - A professional network for individuals interested in AI and robotics research.
3. **International Association for Privacy Professionals (IAPP)**
   - An organization focusing on data privacy, which intersects with ethical considerations in AI.
4. **AI4ALL**
   - A non-profit organization working to increase diversity and inclusion in AI through education and outreach programs.

Tools and Platforms for AI Development:

1. **TensorFlow**
   - An open-source machine learning framework developed by Google for building and deploying AI models.
2. **PyTorch**
   - An open-source deep learning library developed by Facebook, known for its flexibility and ease of use.
3. **Microsoft Azure AI**
   - A cloud-based platform offering a suite of AI tools and services for building and deploying AI solutions.
4. **Google Cloud AI**
   - Provides various AI and machine learning services, including pre-trained models and custom model development.
5. **IBM Watson**
   - A suite of AI-powered tools and services designed for natural language processing, machine learning, and data analysis.

About the Author

Jackson Reed is a seasoned expert in artificial intelligence and technology entrepreneurship, specializing in turning cutting-edge AI innovations into profitable ventures. With years of experience in AI-driven business strategies, Reed has successfully guided numerous startups and established professionals in harnessing the power of AI for financial success.

An acclaimed speaker and consultant, Reed's insights into **monetizing AI**, **AI investment**, and **AI business opportunities** have made him a sought-after authority in the field. His passion for **AI technology** and its transformative potential fuels his commitment to helping others achieve their goals through practical, actionable strategies.

In **"AI Goldmine"**, Jackson Reed shares his expertise and practical wisdom, providing readers with a roadmap to unlock the full potential of artificial intelligence and build lasting wealth.

Notes